AF188465

Impressum
Verlag: BABADADA GmbH, Nedderfeld 112 , 22529 Hamburg
Geschäftsführer / Verlagsleitung: Harald Hof
Druck: Books on Demand GmbH, In de Tarpen 42, 22848 Norderstedt

Imprint
Publisher: BABADADA GmbH, Nedderfeld 112 , 22529 Hamburg, Germany
Managing Director / Publishing direction: Harald Hof
Print: Books on Demand GmbH, In de Tarpen 42, 22848 Norderstedt

school

Schule

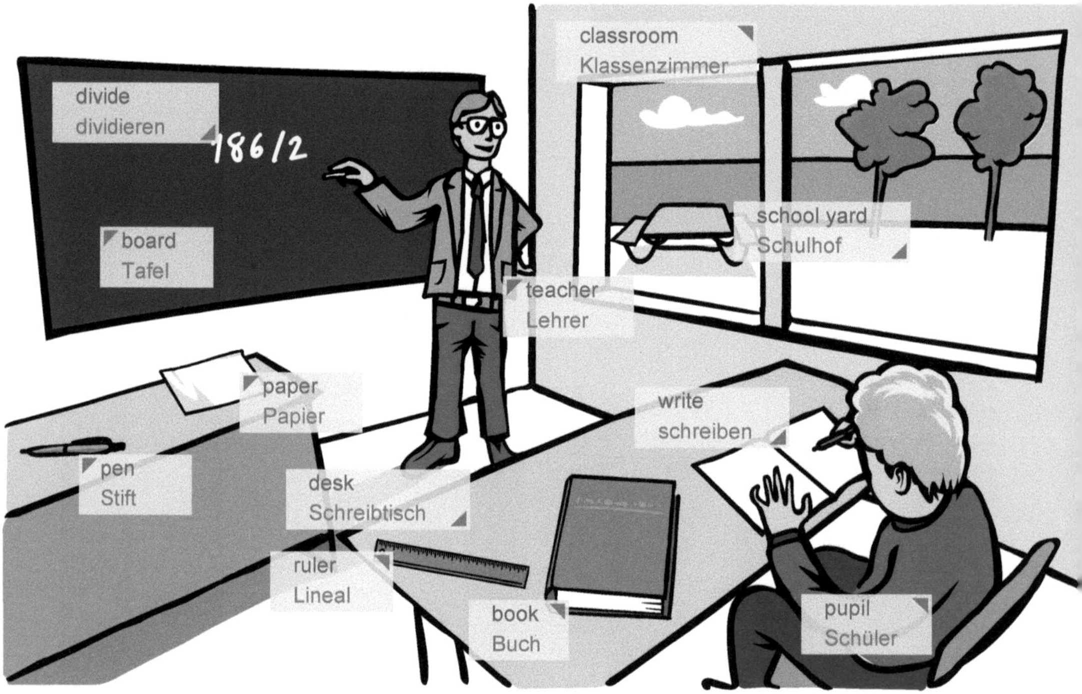

classroom
Klassenzimmer
divide
dividieren
186/2
board
Tafel
school yard
Schulhof
teacher
Lehrer
paper
Papier
write
schreiben
pen
Stift
desk
Schreibtisch
ruler
Lineal
book
Buch
pupil
Schüler

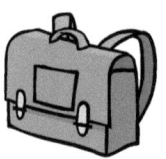

satchel

Schultasche

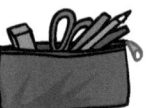

pencil case

Federmappe

pencil

Bleistift

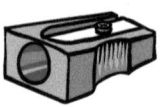

pencil sharpener

Bleistiftspitzer

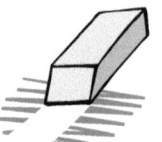

rubber

Radierer

drawing pad

Zeichenblock

drawing

Zeichnung

paintbrush

Pinsel

paint box

Malkasten

scissors

Schere

glue

Klebstoff

exercise book

Übungsheft

homework

Hausübung

number

Zahl

add

addieren

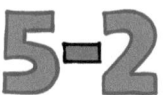

subtract

subtrahieren

multiply

multiplizieren

calculate

rechnen

letter

Buchstabe

alphabet

Alphabet

word

Wort

text

Text

read

lesen

chalk

Kreide

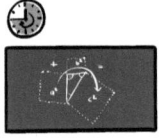

lesson

Unterrichtsstunde

register

Klassenbuch

exam

Prüfung

certificate

Zeugnis

school uniform

Schuluniform

education

Ausbildung

encyclopedia

Lexikon

university

Universität

microscope

Mikroskop

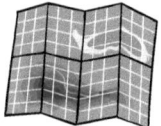

map

Karte

waste-paper basket

Papierkorb

travel
Reise

hotel
Hotel
Grand
hostel
Herberge
ROOMS
bureau de change
Wechselstube
EXCHANGE
car
Auto

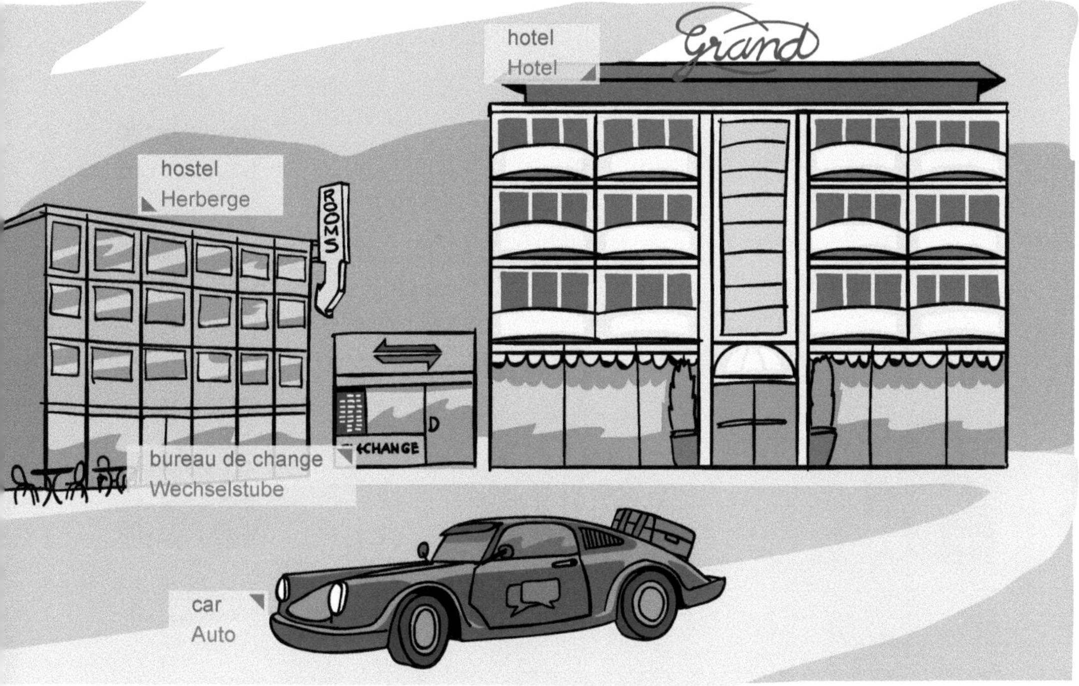

language

Sprache

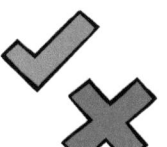

yes / no

ja / nein

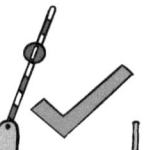

Okay

Okay

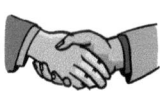

hello

Hallo

translator

Dolmetscherin

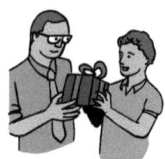

Thank you

Danke

how much is…?

Wie viel kostet …?

I do not understand

Ich verstehe nicht.

problem

Problem

Good evening!

Guten Abend!

Good morning!

Guten Morgen!

Good night!

Gute Nacht!

bye bye

Auf Wiederschaun!

direction

Richtung

luggage

Gepäck

bag

Tasche

backpack

Rucksack

guest

Gast

room

Zimmer

sleeping bag

Schlafsack

tent

Zelt

travel - Reise

tourist information

Touristeninformation

beach

Strand

credit card

Kreditkarte

breakfast

Frühstück

lunch

Mittagessen

dinner

Abendessen

ticket

Fahrkarte

lift

Lift

stamp

Briefmarke

border

Grenze

customs

Zoll

embassy

Botschaft

visa

Visum

passport

Pass

transport
Transport

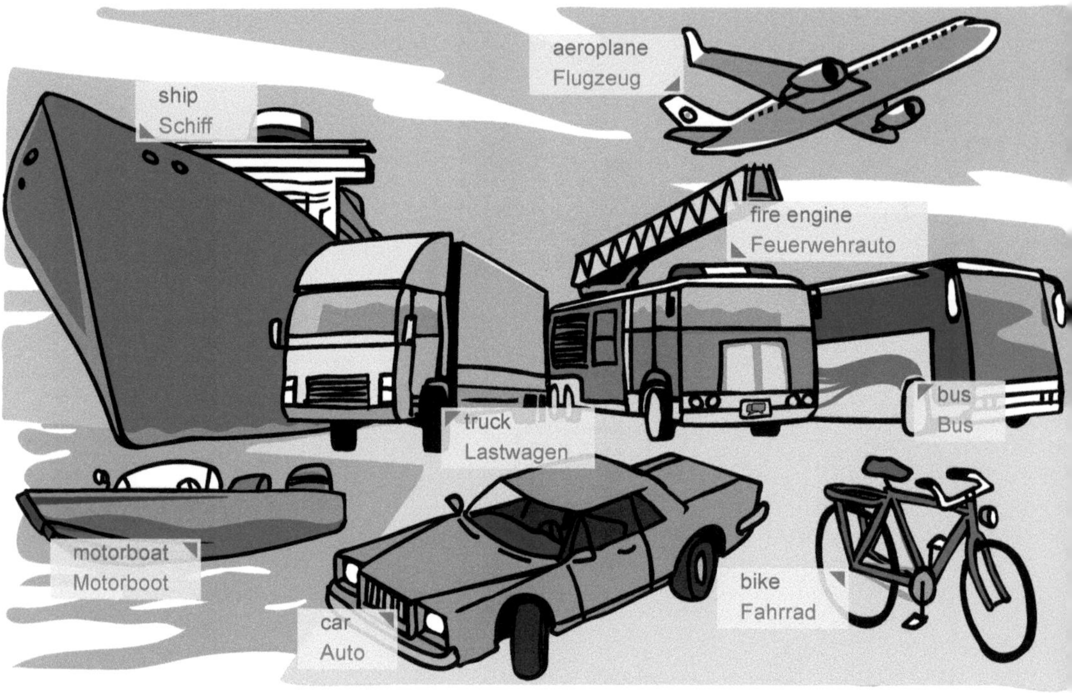
aeroplane
Flugzeug
ship
Schiff
fire engine
Feuerwehrauto
bus
Bus
truck
Lastwagen
motorboat
Motorboot
bike
Fahrrad
car
Auto

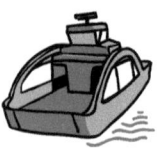

ferry

Fähre

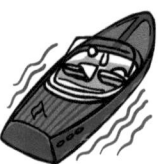

boat

Boot

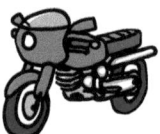

motorbike

Motorrad

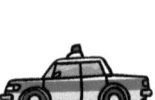

police car

Polizeiauto

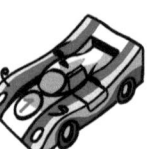

racing car

Rennauto

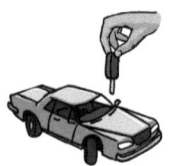

rental car

Mietwagen

car sharing

Carsharing

breakdown truck

Abschleppwagen

refuse truck

Müllwagen

motor

Motor

fuel

Kraftstoff

petrol station

Tankstelle

traffic sign

Verkehrsschild

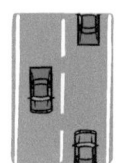

traffic

Verkehr

traffic jam

Stau

car park

Parkplatz

train station

Bahnhof

tracks

Schienen

train

Zug

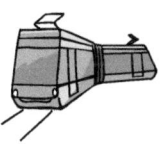

tram

Straßenbahn

carriage

Wagon

helicopter

Hubschrauber

airport

Flughafen

tower

Tower

passenger

Passagier

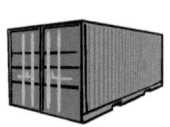

container

Container

carton

Karton

cart

Rollwagen

basket

Korb

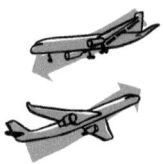

take off / land

starten / landen

city

Stadt

village

Dorf

city centre

Stadtzentrum

house

Haus

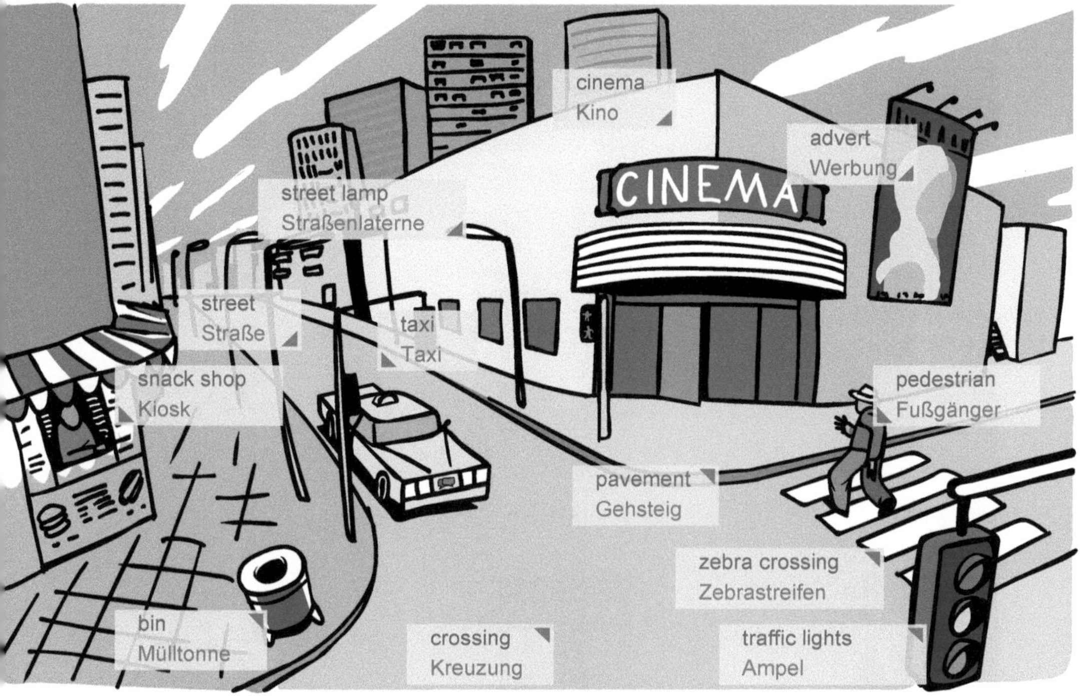

cinema
Kino

advert
Werbung

street lamp
Straßenlaterne

CINEMA

street
Straße

taxi
Taxi

snack shop
Kiosk

pedestrian
Fußgänger

pavement
Gehsteig

zebra crossing
Zebrastreifen

bin
Mülltonne

crossing
Kreuzung

traffic lights
Ampel

hut

Hütte

flat

Wohnung

train station

Bahnhof

town hall

Rathaus

museum

Museum

school

Schule

university

Universität

bank

Bank

hospital

Spital

hotel

Hotel

pharmacy

Apotheke

office

Büro

book shop

Buchhandlung

shop

Geschäft

florist's

Blumenladen

supermarket

Supermarkt

market

Markt

department store

Kaufhaus

fishmonger's

Fischhändler

shopping centre

Einkaufszentrum

harbour

Hafen

city - Stadt

park

Park

bench

Bank

bridge

Brücke

stairs

Stiege

underground

U-Bahn

tunnel

Tunnel

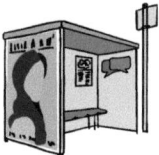

bus stop

Bushaltestelle

bar

Bar

restaurant

Restaurant

postbox

Briefkasten

street sign

Straßenschild

parking meter

Parkuhr

zoo

Zoo

swimming pool

Badeanstalt

mosque

Moschee

farm

Bauernhof

pollution

Umweltverschmutzung

graveyard

Friedhof

church

Kirche

playground

Spielplatz

temple

Tempel

landscape
Landschaft

signpost
Wegweiser

way
Weg

meadow
Wiese

stone
Stein

hiker
Wanderer

tree
Baum

river
Fluss

grass
Gras

flower
Blume

valley

Tal

hill

Hügel

lake

See

forest

Wald

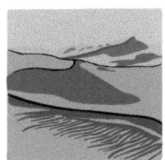

desert

Wüste

volcano

Vulkan

castle

Schloss

rainbow

Regenbogen

mushroom

Pilz

palm tree

Palme

mosquito

Moskito

fly

Fliege

ant

Ameise

bee

Biene

spider

Spinne

beetle
Käfer

frog
Frosch

squirrel
Eichhörnchen

hedgehog
Igel

hare
Hase

owl
Eule

bird
Vogel

swan
Schwan

boar
Wildschwein

deer
Hirsch

moose
Elch

dam
Staudamm

wind turbine
Windrad

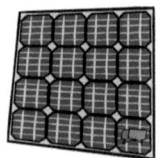

solar panel
Solarmodul

climate
Klima

restaurant
Restaurant

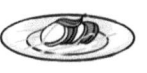

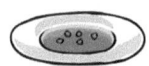

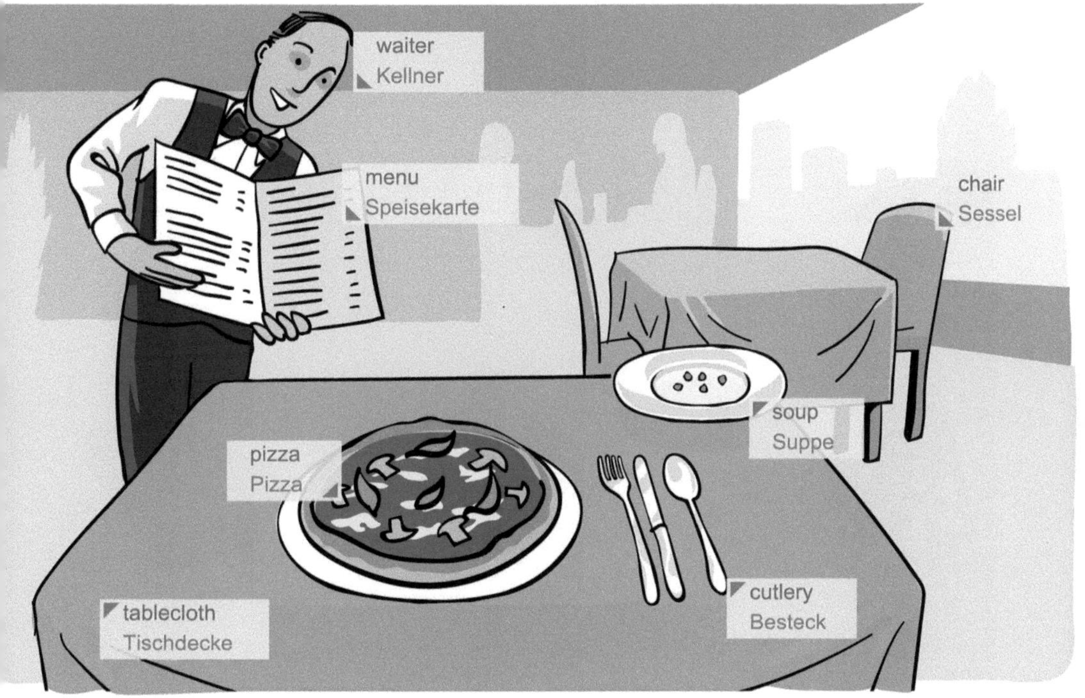
waiter
Kellner
menu
Speisekarte
chair
Sessel
soup
Suppe
pizza
Pizza
cutlery
Besteck
tablecloth
Tischdecke

starter

Vorspeise

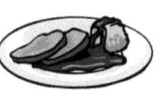

main course

Hauptgericht

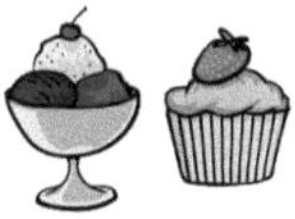

dessert

Nachspeise

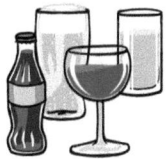

drinks

Getränke

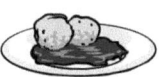

food

Essen

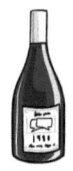

bottle

Flasche

fast food

Fastfood

street food

Streetfood

teapot

Teekanne

sugar bowl

Zuckerdose

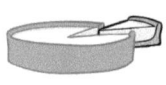

portion

Portion

espresso machine

Espressomaschine

high chair

Kinderstuhl

bill

Rechnung

tray

Tablett

knife

Messer

fork

Gabel

spoon

Löffel

teaspoon

Teelöffel

serviette

Serviette

glass

Glas

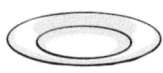

plate

Teller

soup plate

Suppenteller

saucer

Untertasse

sauce

Sauce

salt pot

Salzstreuer

pepper mill

Pfeffermühle

vinegar

Essig

oil

Öl

spices

Gewürze

ketchup

Ketchup

mustard

Senf

mayonnaise

Mayonnaise

supermarket

Supermarkt

special offer
Angebot
FOR
customer
Kunde
dairy
Milchprodukte
fruit
Obst
trolley
Einkaufswagen

BUTCHERS

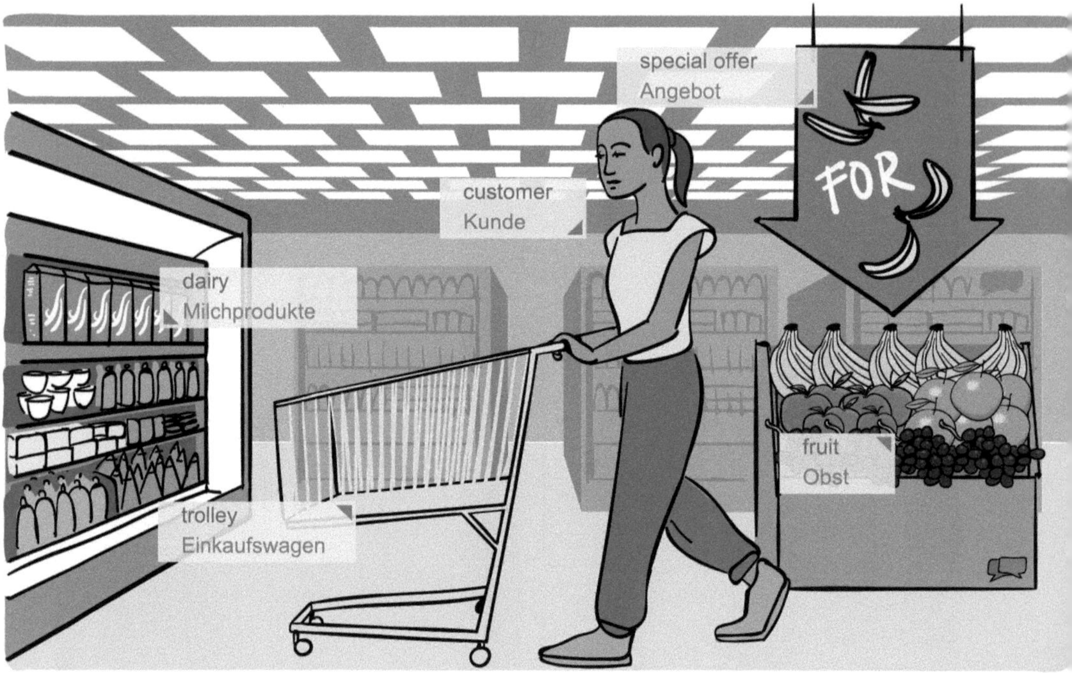

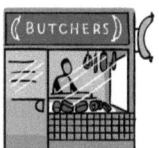

butcher´s

Schlachterei

BAKERY

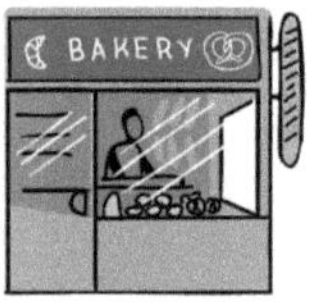

baker´s

Bäckerei

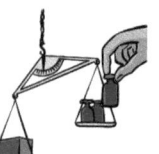

weigh

wiegen

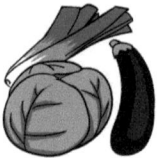

vegetables

Gemüse

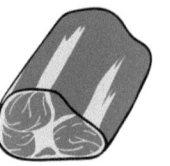

meat

Fleisch

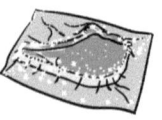

frozen food

Tiefkühlkost

cold meat

Aufschnitt

tinned food

Konserven

washing powder

Waschmittel

sweets

Süßigkeiten

household products

Haushaltsartikel

cleaning products

Reinigungsmittel

salesperson

Verkäuferin

till

Kassa

cashier

Kassiererin

shopping list

Einkaufsliste

opening hours

Öffnungszeiten

wallet

Brieftasche

credit card

Kreditkarte

bag

Tasche

plastic bag

Plastiktüte

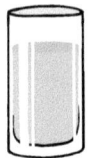

water

Wasser

juice

Saft

milk

Milch

coke

Cola

wine

Wein

beer

Bier

alcohol

Alkohol

cocoa

Kakao

tea

Tee

coffee

Kaffee

espresso

Espresso

cappuccino

Cappuccino

banana
Banane

apple
Apfel

orange
Orange

melon
Melone

lemon
Zitrone

carrot
Karotte

garlic
Knoblauch

bamboo
Bambus

onion
Zwiebel

mushroom
Pilz

nuts
Nüsse

noodles
Nudeln

spaghetti

Spaghetti

rice

Reis

salad

Salat

chips

Pommes frites

fried potatoes

Bratkartoffeln

pizza

Pizza

hamburger

Hamburger

sandwich

Sandwich

cutlet

Schnitzel

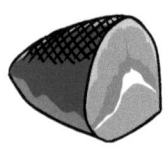

ham

Schinken

salami

Salami

sausage

Wurst

chicken

Huhn

roast

Braten

fish

Fisch

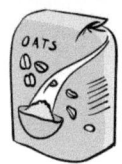

porridge oats

Haferflocken

muesli

Müsli

cornflakes

Cornflakes

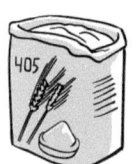

flour

Mehl

croissant

Croissant

bread roll

Semmel

bread

Brot

toast

Toast

biscuits

Kekse

butter

Butter

curd

Topfen

cake

Kuchen

egg

Ei

fried egg

Spiegelei

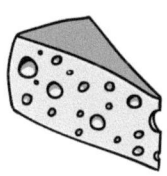

cheese

Käse

ice cream

Eiscreme

sugar

Zucker

honey

Honig

jam

Marmelade

chocolate spread

Schokoladenaufstrich

curry

Curry

goat

Ziege

cow

Kuh

calf

Kalb

pig

Schwein

piglet

Ferkel

bull

Stier

goose

Gans

duck

Ente

chick

Küken

hen

Huhn

cock

Hahn

rat

Ratte

cat

Katze

mouse

Maus

ox

Ochse

dog

Hund

doghouse

Hundehütte

garden hose

Gartenschlauch

watering can

Gießkanne

scythe

Sense

plough

Pflug

farm - Bauernhof

sickle

Sichel

hoe

Hacke

pitchfork

Mistgabel

axe

Axt

wheelbarrow

Schubkarre

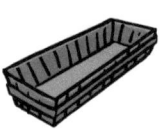

trough

Trog

milk can

Milchkanne

sack

Sack

fence

Zaun

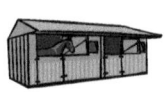

stable

Stall

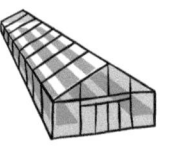

greenhouse

Treibhaus

soil

Boden

seed

Saat

fertilizer

Dünger

combine harvester

Mähdrescher

harvest
ernten

harvest
Ernte

yams
Yamswurzel

wheat
Weizen

soy
Soja

potato
Erdapfel

corn
Mais

rapeseed
Raps

fruit tree
Obstbaum

cassava
Maniok

cereals
Getreide

living room

Wohnzimmer

bathroom

Badezimmer

kitchen

Küche

bedroom

Schlafzimmer

child's room

Kinderzimmer

dining room

Esszimmer

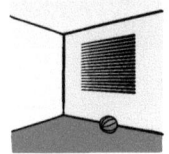

floor

Boden

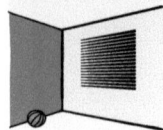

wall

Wand

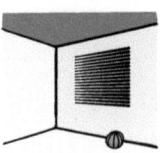

ceiling

Decke

cellar

Keller

sauna

Sauna

balcony

Balkon

terrace

Terrasse

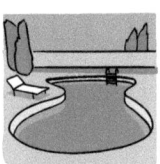

pool

Schwimmbad

lawn mower

Rasenmäher

sheet

Bettbezug

bedspread

Bettdecke

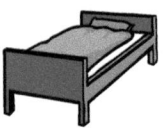

bed

Bett

broom

Besen

bucket

Kübel

switch

Schalter

living room
Wohnzimmer

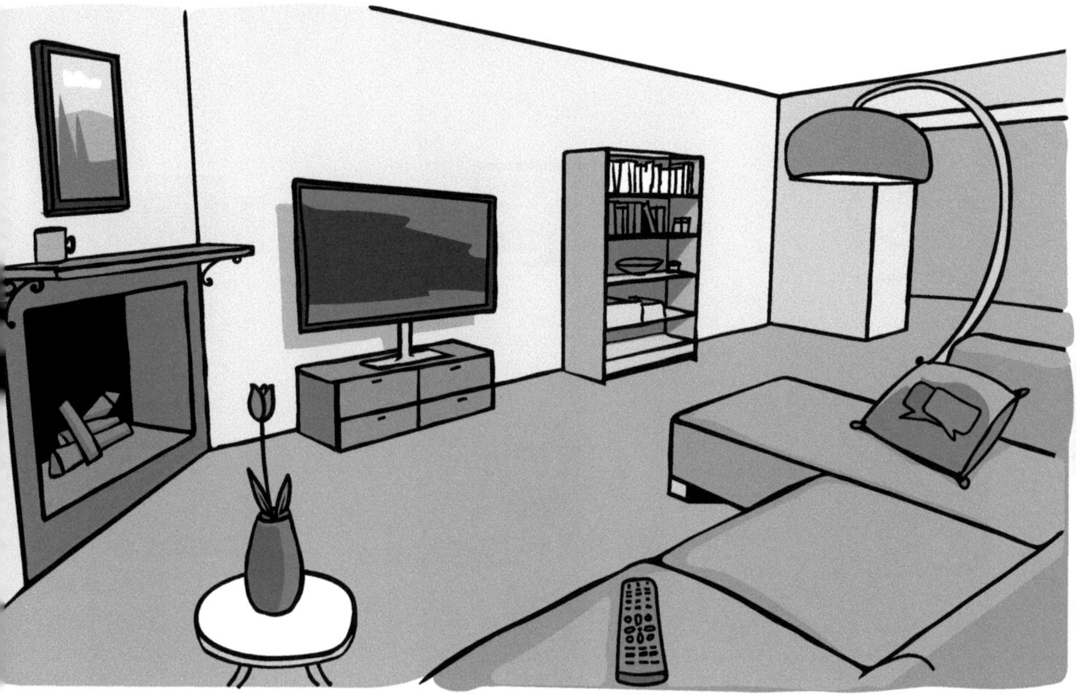

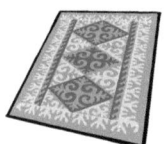

carpet

Teppich

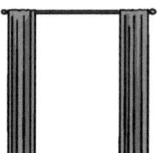

curtain

Vorhang

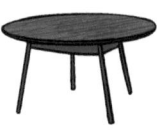

table

Tisch

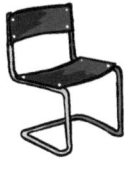

chair

Sessel

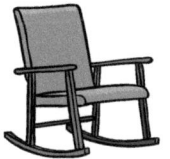

rocking chair

Schaukelstuhl

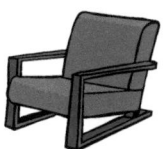

armchair

Sessel

book

Buch

blanket

Decke

decoration

Dekoration

firewood

Feuerholz

film

Film

hi-fi equipment

Stereoanlage

key

Schlüssel

newspaper

Zeitung

painting

Gemälde

poster

Poster

radio

Radio

notepad

Notizblock

hoover

Staubsauger

cactus

Kaktus

candle

Kerze

kitchen
Küche

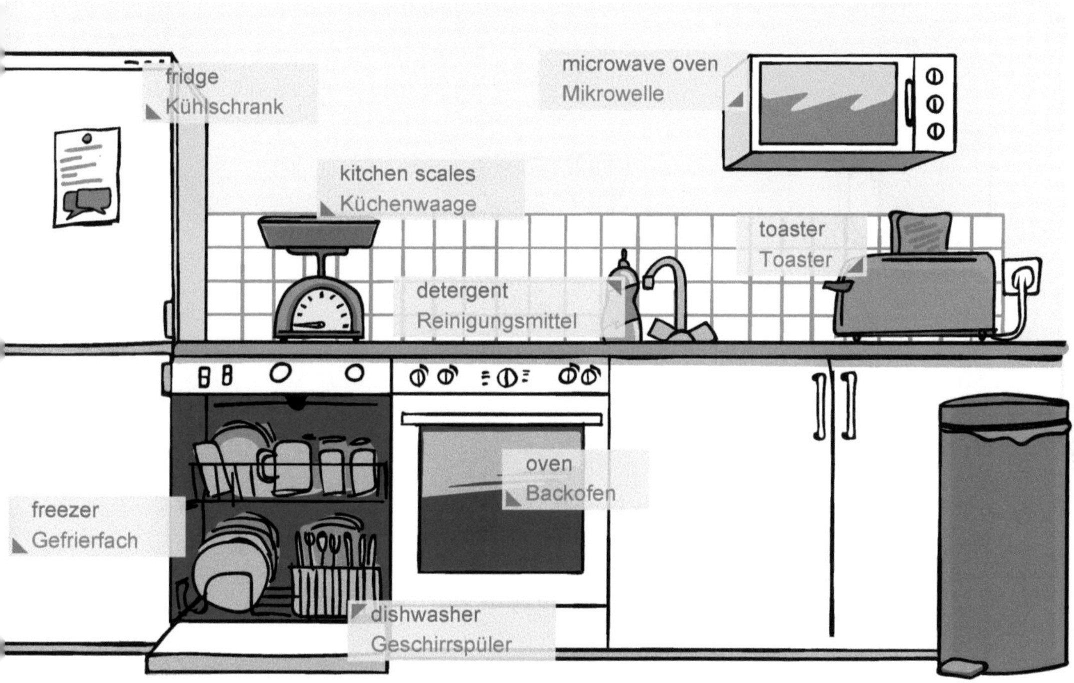

fridge
Kühlschrank
microwave oven
Mikrowelle
kitchen scales
Küchenwaage
toaster
Toaster
detergent
Reinigungsmittel
oven
Backofen
freezer
Gefrierfach
dishwasher
Geschirrspüler

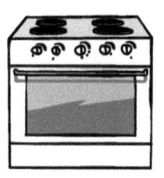

cooker
Herd

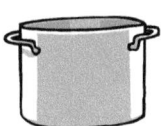

pot
Topf

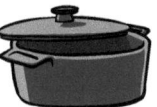

cast-iron pot
Eisentopf

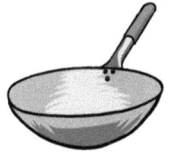

wok / kadai
Wok / Kadai

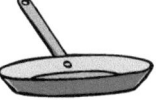

pan
Pfanne

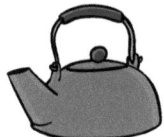

kettle
Wasserkocher

steamer

Dampfgarer

baking tray

Backblech

crockery

Geschirr

mug

Becher

bowl

Schale

chopsticks

Essstäbchen

ladle

Schöpflöffel

spatula

Pfannenwender

whisk

Schneebesen

strainer

Kochsieb

sieve

Sieb

grater

Reibe

mortar

Mörser

barbecue

Grill

open fire

Kaminfeuer

chopping board

Schneidebrett

rolling pin

Nudelholz

corkscrew

Korkenzieher

can

Dose

can opener

Dosenöffner

pot holder

Topflappen

sink

Waschbecken

brush

Bürste

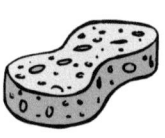

sponge

Schwamm

blender

Mixer

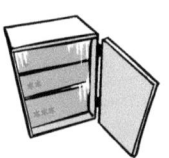

deep freezer

Gefriertruhe

baby bottle

Babyflasche

tap

Wasserhahn

bathroom
Badezimmer

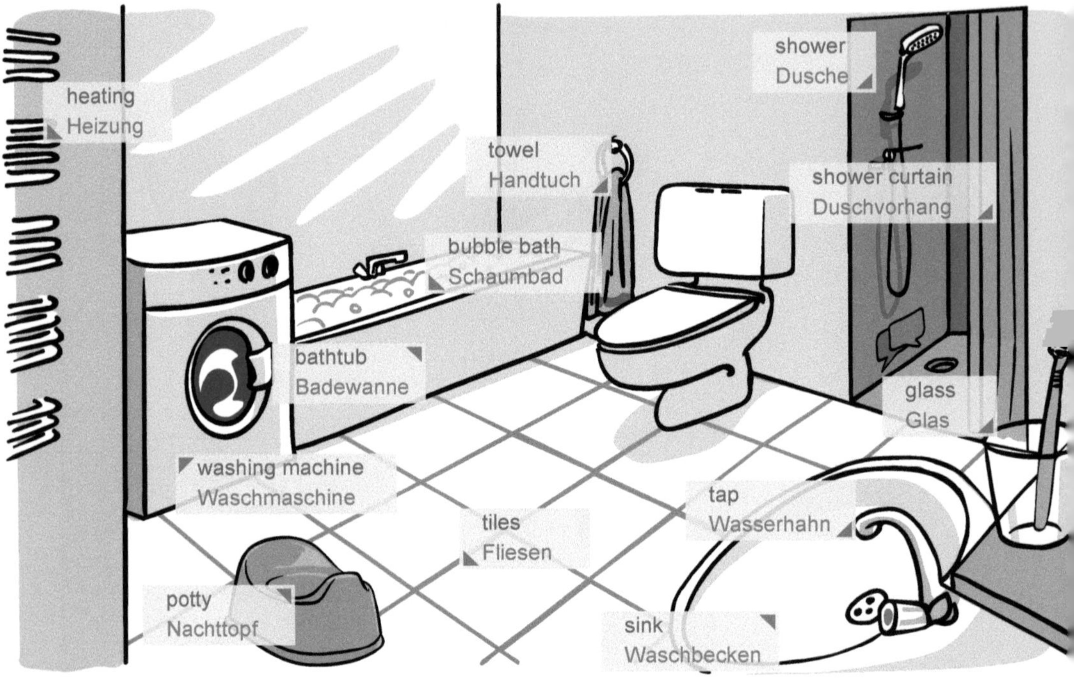

heating
Heizung
shower
Dusche
towel
Handtuch
shower curtain
Duschvorhang
bubble bath
Schaumbad
bathtub
Badewanne
glass
Glas
washing machine
Waschmaschine
tap
Wasserhahn
tiles
Fliesen
potty
Nachttopf
sink
Waschbecken

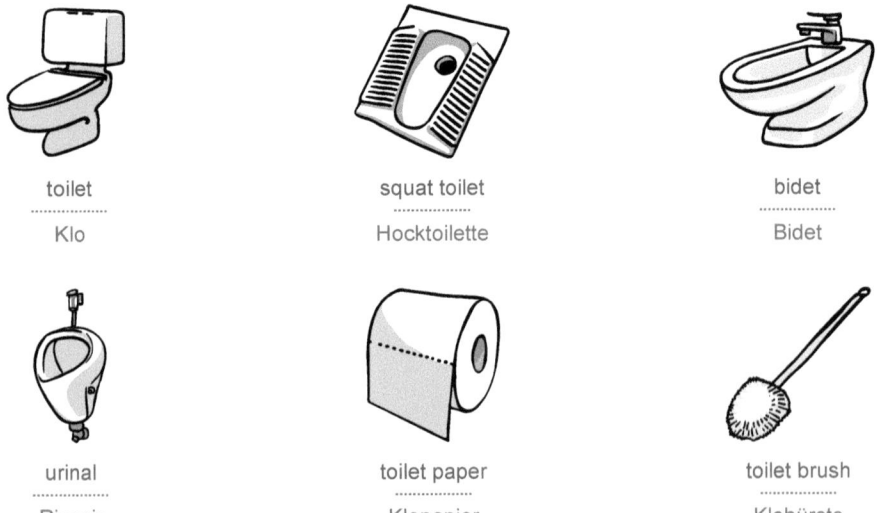

toilet

Klo

squat toilet

Hocktoilette

bidet

Bidet

urinal

Pissoir

toilet paper

Klopapier

toilet brush

Klobürste

toothbrush

Zahnbürste

toothpaste

Zahnpasta

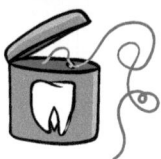

dental floss

Zahnseide

wash

waschen

handheld shower

Handbrause

douche

Intimdusche

basin

Waschschüssel

back brush

Rückenbürste

soap

Seife

shower gel

Duschgel

shampoo

Shampoo

flannel

Waschlappen

drain

Abfluss

cream

Creme

deodorant

Deodorant

mirror

Spiegel

hand mirror

Kosmetikspiegel

razor

Rasierer

shaving foam

Rasierschaum

aftershave

Rasierwasser

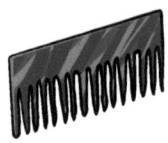

comb

Kamm

brush

Bürste

hair dryer

Föhn

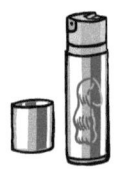

hairspray

Haarspray

makeup

Makeup

lipstick

Lippenstift

nail varnish

Nagellack

cotton wool

Watte

nail scissors

Nagelschere

perfume

Parfum

bathroom - Badezimmer

washbag

Kulturbeutel

stool

Hocker

weighing scale

Waage

bathrobe

Bademantel

rubber gloves

Gummihandschuhe

tampon

Tampon

sanitary towel

Damenbinde

chemical toilet

Chemietoilette

child's room
Kinderzimmer

alarm clock
Wecker
cuddly toy
Kuscheltier
toy car
Spielzeugauto
rattle
Rassel
doll's house
Puppenhaus
present
Geschenk

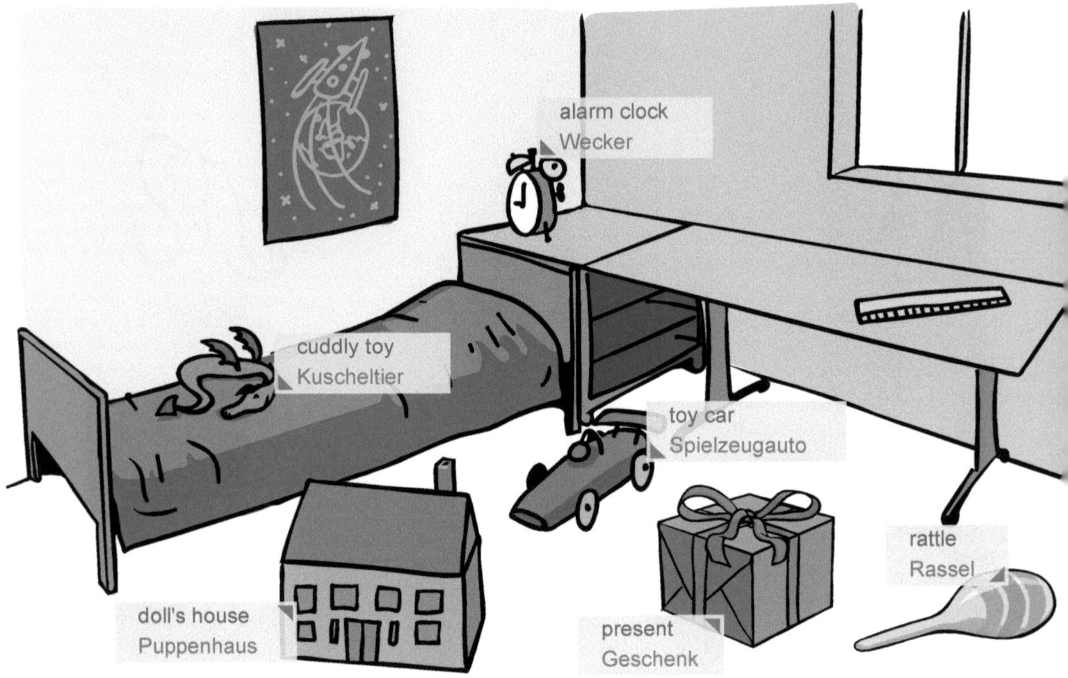

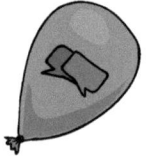

balloon

Ballon

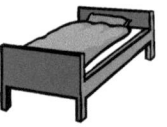

bed

Bett

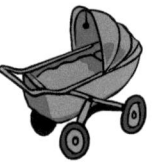

pram

Kinderwagen

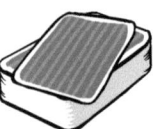

deck of cards

Kartenspiel

jigsaw

Puzzle

SUPER
MEGA

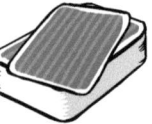

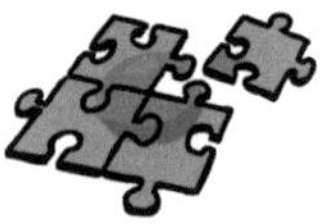

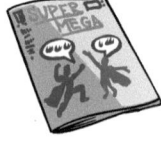

comic

Comic

lego bricks

Legosteine

building blocks

Bausteine

action figure

Actionfigur

babygrow

Strampelanzug

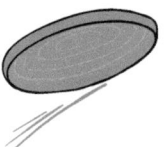

frisbee

Frisbee

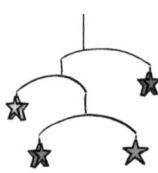

mobile

Mobile

board game

Brettspiel

dice

Würfel

model train set

Modelleisenbahn

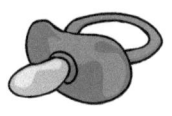

dummy

Schnuller

party

Party

picture book

Bilderbuch

ball

Ball

doll

Puppe

play

spielen

sandpit

Sandkasten

swing

Schaukel

toys

Spielzeug

video game console

Spielkonsole

tricycle

Dreirad

teddy bear

Teddy

wardrobe

Kleiderschrank

clothing

Kleidung

socks

Socken

stockings

Strümpfe

tights

Strumpfhose

scarf
Schal

belt
Gürtel

umbrella
Regenschirm

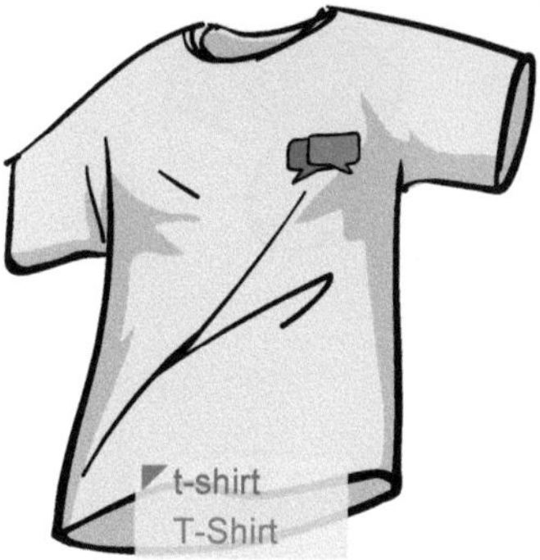

t-shirt
T-Shirt

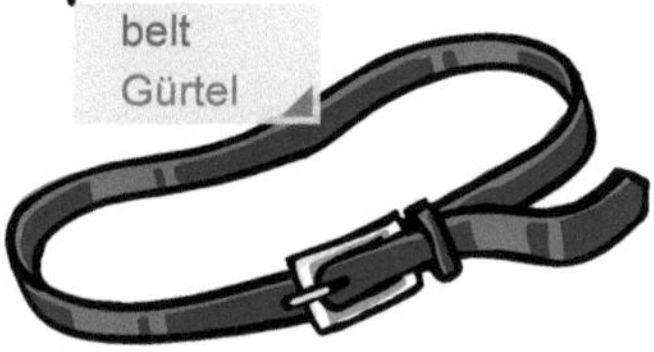

trainers
Turnschuhe

boots
Stiefel

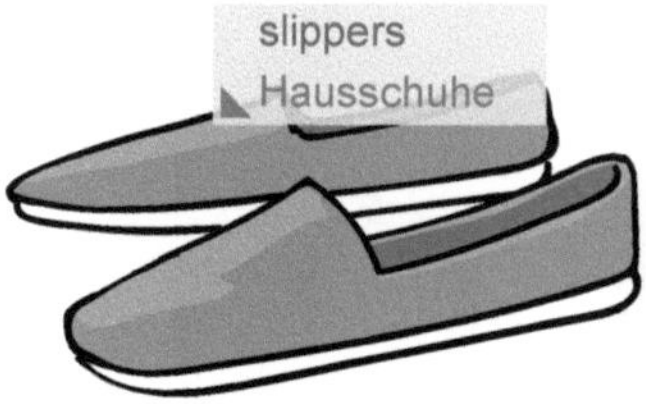

slippers
Hausschuhe

sandals
....
Sandalen

shoes
....
Schuhe

rubber boots
....
Gummistiefel

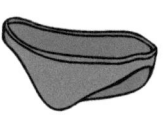

underpants
....
Unterhose

bra
....
Büstenhalter

vest
....
Unterhemd

body

Body

trousers

Hose

jeans

Jeans

skirt

Rock

blouse

Bluse

shirt

Hemd

pullover

Pullover

hoodie

Kapuzenpullover

blazer

Blazer

jacket

Jacke

coat

Mantel

raincoat

Regenmantel

costume

Kostüm

dress

Kleid

wedding dress

Hochzeitskleid

suit

Anzug

nightgown

Nachthemd

pyjamas

Pyjama

sari

Sari

headscarf

Kopftuch

turban

Turban

burqa

Burka

kaftan

Kaftan

abaya

Abaya

swimsuit

Badeanzug

trunks

Badehose

shorts

kurze Hose

tracksuit

Jogginganzug

apron

Schürze

gloves

Handschuhe

button

Knopf

glasses

Brille

bracelet

Armband

necklace

Halskette

ring

Ring

earring

Ohrring

cap

Mütze

coat hanger

Kleiderbügel

hat

Hut

tie

Krawatte

zip

Reißverschluss

helmet

Helm

braces

Hosenträger

school uniform

Schuluniform

uniform

Uniform

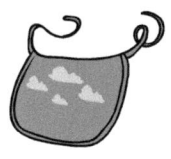

bib

Lätzchen

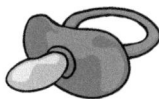

dummy

Schnuller

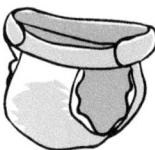

nappy

Windel

office
Büro

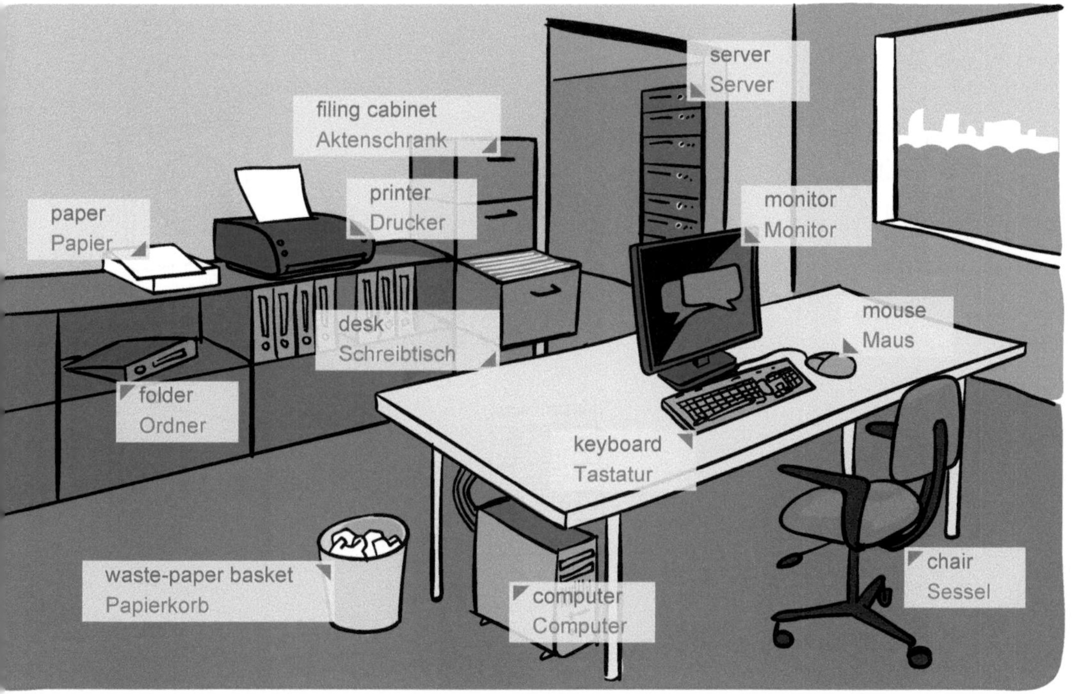

server
Server
filing cabinet
Aktenschrank
printer
Drucker
paper
Papier
monitor
Monitor
mouse
Maus
desk
Schreibtisch
folder
Ordner
keyboard
Tastatur
waste-paper basket
Papierkorb
computer
Computer
chair
Sessel

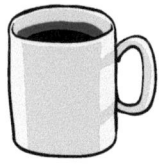

coffee mug

Kaffeebecher

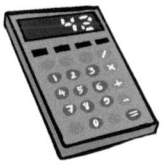

calculator

Taschenrechner

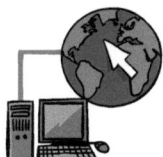

internet

Internet

laptop

Laptop

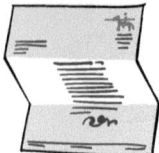

letter

Brief

message

Nachricht

mobile

Handy

network

Netzwerk

photocopier

Kopierer

software

Software

telephone

Telefon

plug socket

Steckdose

fax machine

Fax

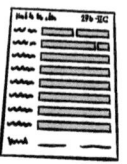

form

Formular

document

Dokument

office - Büro

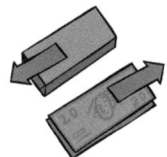

buy

kaufen

pay

bezahlen

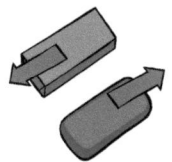

trade

handeln

money

Geld

dollar

Dollar

euro

Euro

yen

Yen

rouble

Rubel

Swiss franc

Franken

renminbi yuan

Renminbi Yuan

rupee

Rupie

cashpoint

Bankomat

bureau de change

Wechselstube

gold

Gold

silver

Silber

oil

Öl

energy

Energie

price

Preis

contract

Vertrag

tax

Steuer

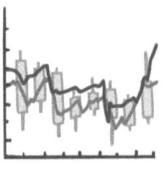

stock

Aktie

work

arbeiten

employee

Angestellte

employer

Arbeitgeber

factory

Fabrik

shop

Geschäft

economy - Wirtschaft

occupations
Berufe

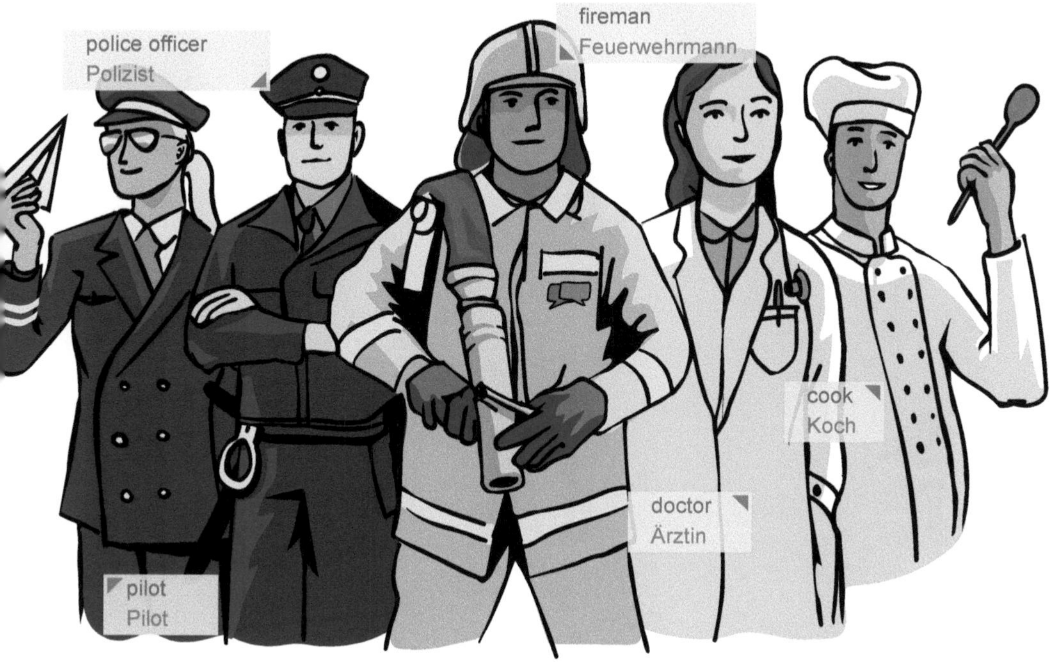

police officer
Polizist
fireman
Feuerwehrmann
cook
Koch
doctor
Ärztin
pilot
Pilot

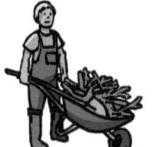

gardener
Gärtner

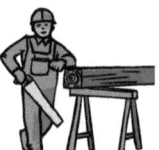

carpenter
Tischler

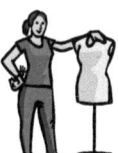

seamstress
Schneiderin

judge
Richter

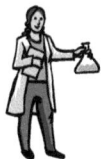

chemist
Chemikerin

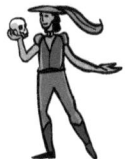

actor
Schauspieler

bus driver

Busfahrer

taxi driver

Taxifahrer

fisherman

Fischer

cleaning lady

Putzfrau

roofer

Dachdecker

waiter

Kellner

hunter

Jäger

painter

Maler

baker

Bäcker

electrician

Elektriker

builder

Bauarbeiter

engineer

Ingenieur

butcher

Schlachter

plumber

Installateur

postman

Briefträgerin

soldier

Soldat

architect

Architekt

cashier

Kassiererin

florist

Blumenhändlerin

hairdresser

Friseur

conductor

Schaffner

mechanic

Mechaniker

captain

Kapitän

dentist

Zahnärztin

scientist

Wissenschaftler

rabbi

Rabbi

imam

Imam

monk

Mönch

clergyman

Pfarrer

tools
Werkzeuge

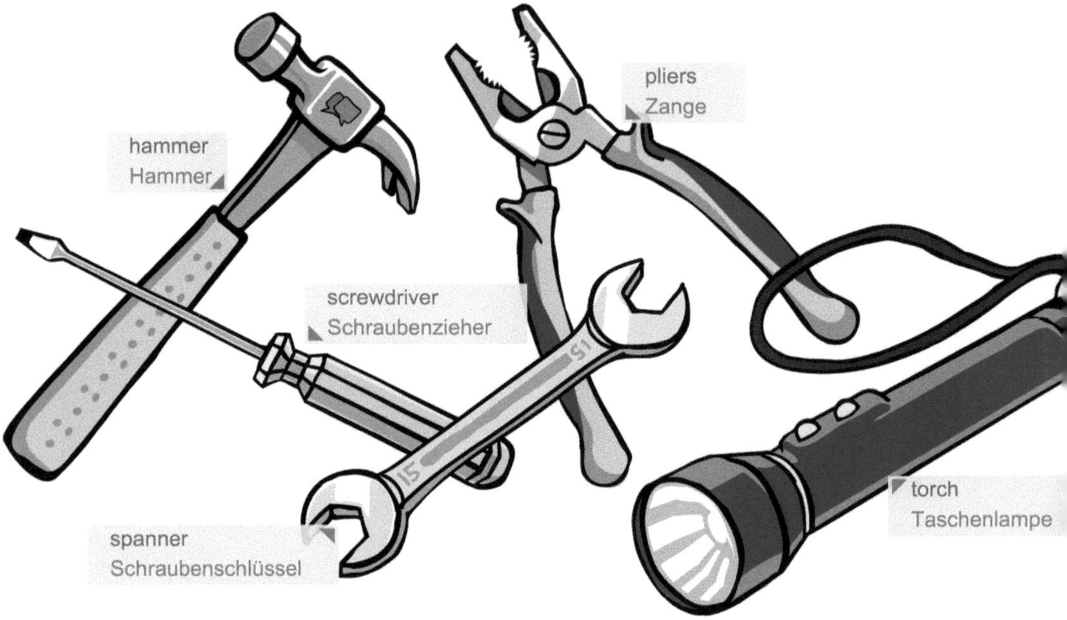
pliers
Zange
hammer
Hammer
screwdriver
Schraubenzieher
torch
Taschenlampe
spanner
Schraubenschlüssel

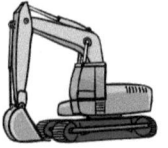

digger

Bagger

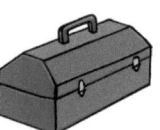

toolbox

Werkzeugkasten

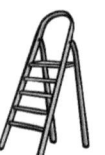

ladder

Leiter

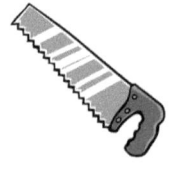

saw

Säge

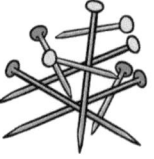

nails

Nägel

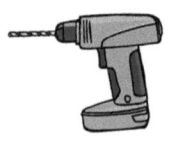

drill

Bohrer

repair
reparieren

shovel
Schaufel

Damn!
Scheiße!

dustpan
Kehrschaufel

paint pot
Farbtopf

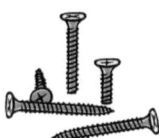

screws
Schrauben

musical instruments
Musikinstrumente

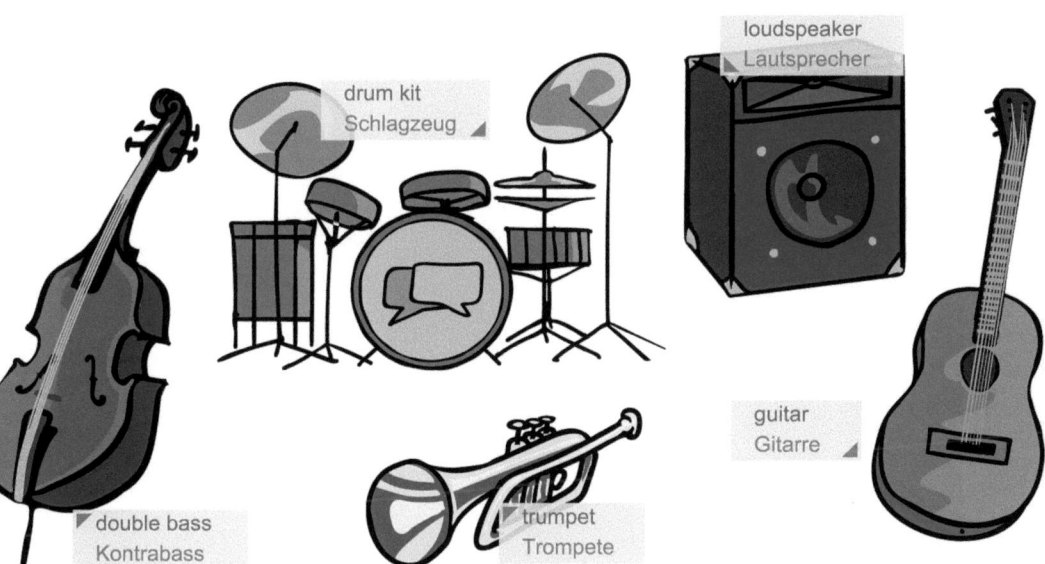

loudspeaker
Lautsprecher

drum kit
Schlagzeug

guitar
Gitarre

double bass
Kontrabass

trumpet
Trompete

piano

Klavier

violin

Violine

bass

Bass

timpani

Pauke

drums

Trommeln

keyboard

Tastatur

saxophone

Saxophon

flute

Flöte

microphone

Mikrofon

zoo

Zoo

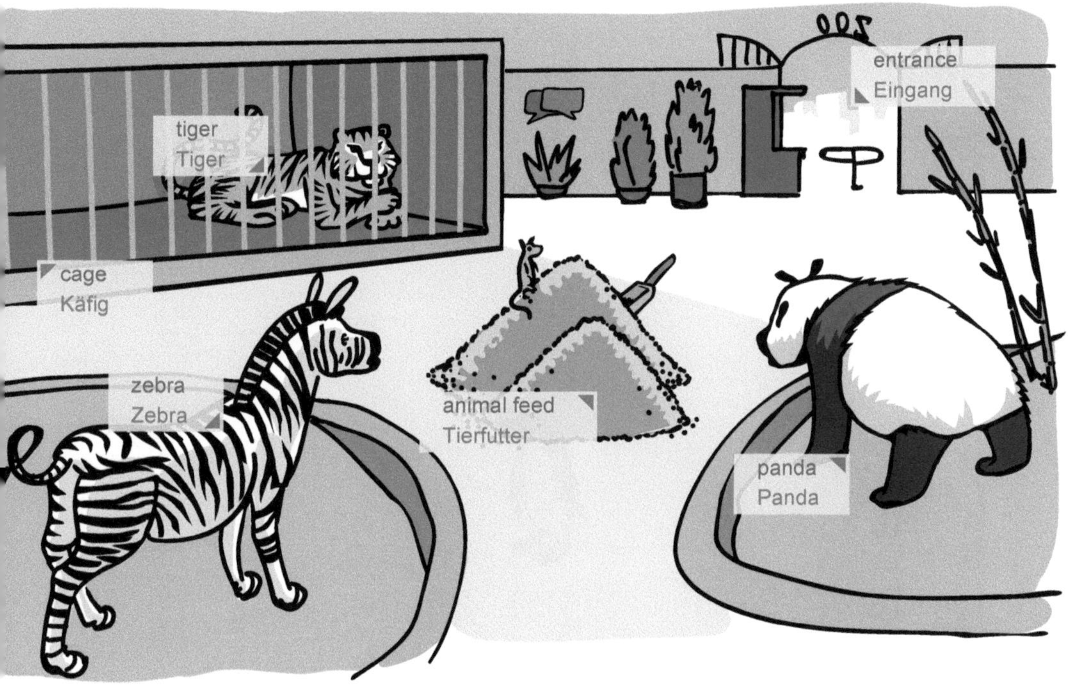

tiger
Tiger
entrance
Eingang
cage
Käfig
zebra
Zebra
animal feed
Tierfutter
panda
Panda

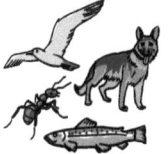

animals

Tiere

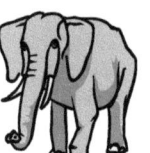

elephant

Elefant

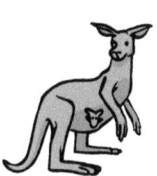

kangaroo

Känguru

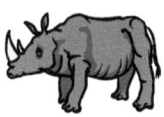

rhino

Nashorn

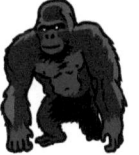

gorilla

Gorilla

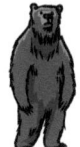

bear

Bär

camel

Kamel

ostrich

Strauß

lion

Löwe

monkey

Affe

flamingo

Flamingo

parrot

Papagei

polar bear

Eisbär

penguin

Pinguin

shark

Hai

peacock

Pfau

snake

Schlange

crocodile

Krokodil

zookeeper

Zoowärter

seal

Robbe

jaguar

Jaguar

pony
Pony

leopard
Leopard

hippo
Nilpferd

giraffe
Giraffe

eagle
Adler

boar
Wildschwein

fish
Fisch

turtle
Schildkröte

walrus
Walross

fox
Fuchs

gazelle
Gazelle

American football
American Football

cycling
Radfahren

tennis
Tennis

basketball
Basketball

swimming
Schwimmen

boxing
Boxen

ice hockey
Eishockey

football
Fußball

badminton
Badminton

athletics
Leichtathletik

handball
Handball

skiing
Skifahren

polo
Polo

jump
springen

laugh
lachen

hug
umarmen

walk
gehen

sing
singen

dream
träumen

pray
beten

kiss
küssen

write

schreiben

draw

zeichnen

show

zeigen

push

drücken

give

geben

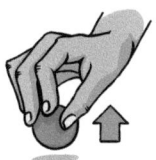

take

nehmen

have

haben

do

machen

be

sein

stand

stehen

run

laufen

pull

ziehen

throw

werfen

fall

fallen

lie

liegen

wait

warten

carry

tragen

sit

sitzen

get dressed

anziehen

sleep

schlafen

wake up

aufwachen

look at

ansehen

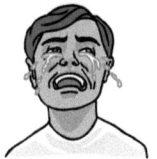

cry

weinen

stroke

streicheln

comb

frisieren

talk

reden

understand

verstehen

ask

fragen

listen

hören

drink

trinken

eat

essen

tidy up

zusammenräumen

love

lieben

cook

kochen

drive

fahren

fly

fliegen

sail

segeln

calculate

rechnen

read

lesen

learn

lernen

work

arbeiten

marry

heiraten

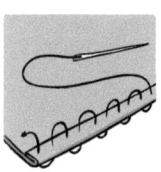

sew

nähen

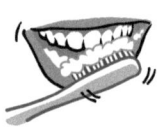

brush teeth

Zähne putzen

kill

töten

smoke

rauchen

send

senden

activities - Aktivitäten

family
Familie

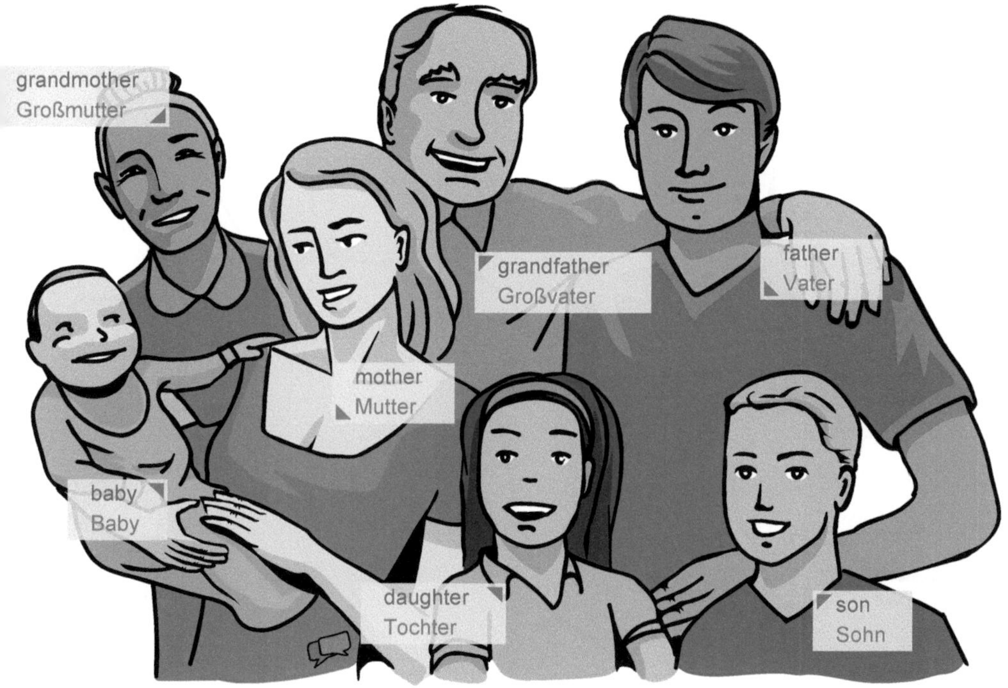
grandmother
Großmutter
grandfather
Großvater
father
Vater
mother
Mutter
baby
Baby
daughter
Tochter
son
Sohn

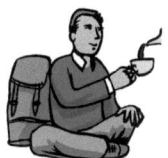

guest

Gast

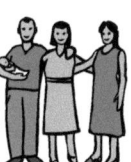

aunt

Tante

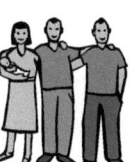

uncle

Onkel

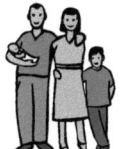

brother

Bruder

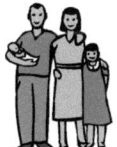

sister

Schwester

body
Körper

forehead
Stirn
eye
Auge
face
Gesicht
chin
Kinn
breast
Brust
finger
Finger
hand
Hand
arm
Arm
shoulder
Schulter
leg
Bein

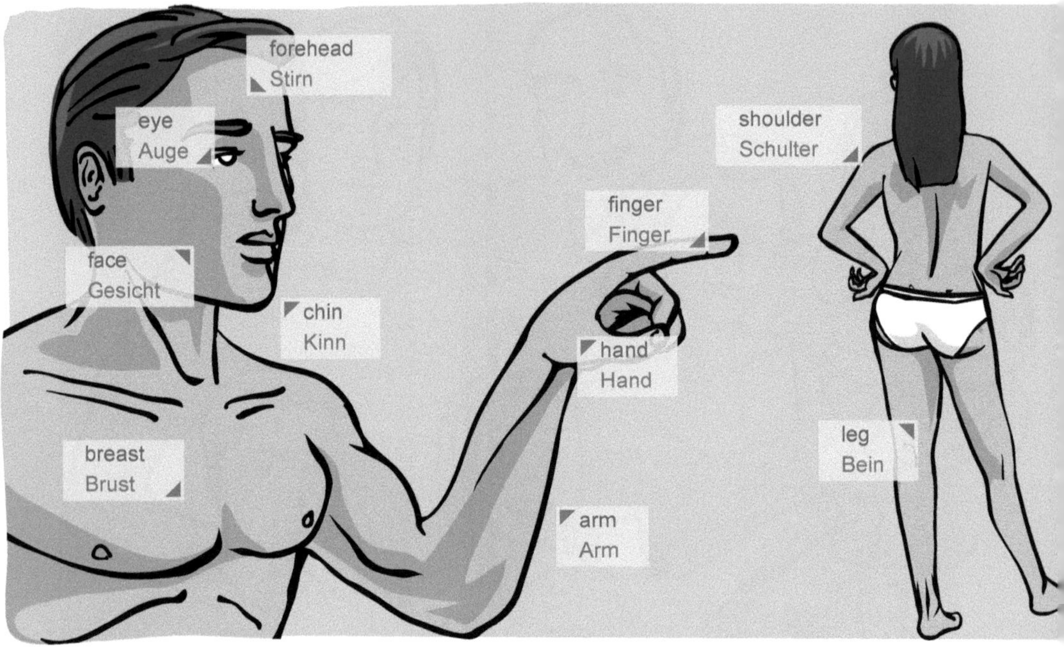

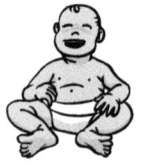

baby
Baby

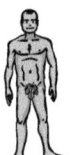

man
Mann

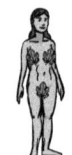

woman
Frau

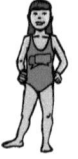

girl
Mädchen

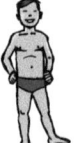

boy
Junge

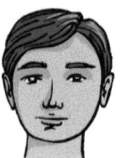

head
Kopf

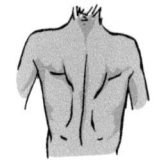

back

Rücken

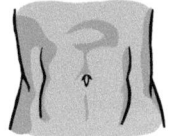

belly

Bauch

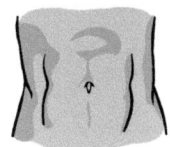

belly button

Nabel

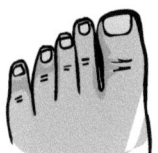

toe

Zeh

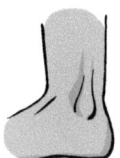

heel

Ferse

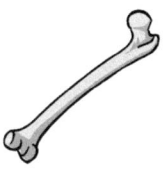

bone

Knochen

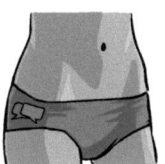

hip

Hüfte

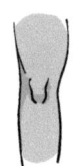

knee

Knie

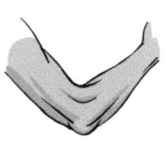

elbow

Ellbogen

nose

Nase

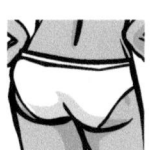

bottom

Gesäß

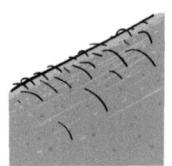

skin

Haut

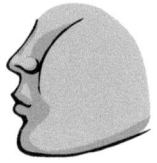

cheek

Wange

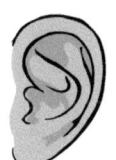

ear

Ohr

lip

Lippe

mouth

Mund

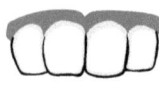

tooth

Zahn

tongue

Zunge

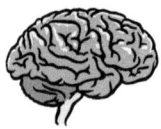

brain

Gehirn

heart

Herz

muscle

Muskel

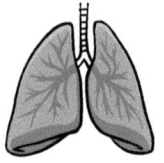

lung

Lunge

liver

Leber

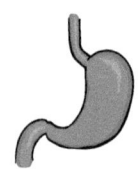

stomach

Magen

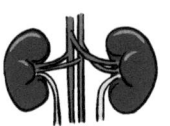

kidneys

Nieren

sex

Geschlechtsverkehr

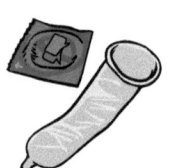

condom

Kondom

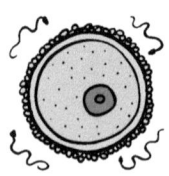

ovum

Eizelle

semen

Sperma

pregnancy

Schwangerschaft

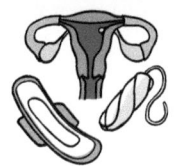

menstruation

Menstruation

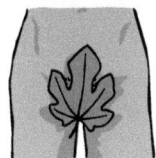

vagina

Vagina

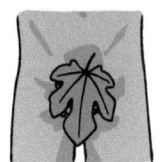

penis

Penis

eyebrow

Augenbraue

hair

Haar

neck

Hals

body - Körper

hospital
Spital

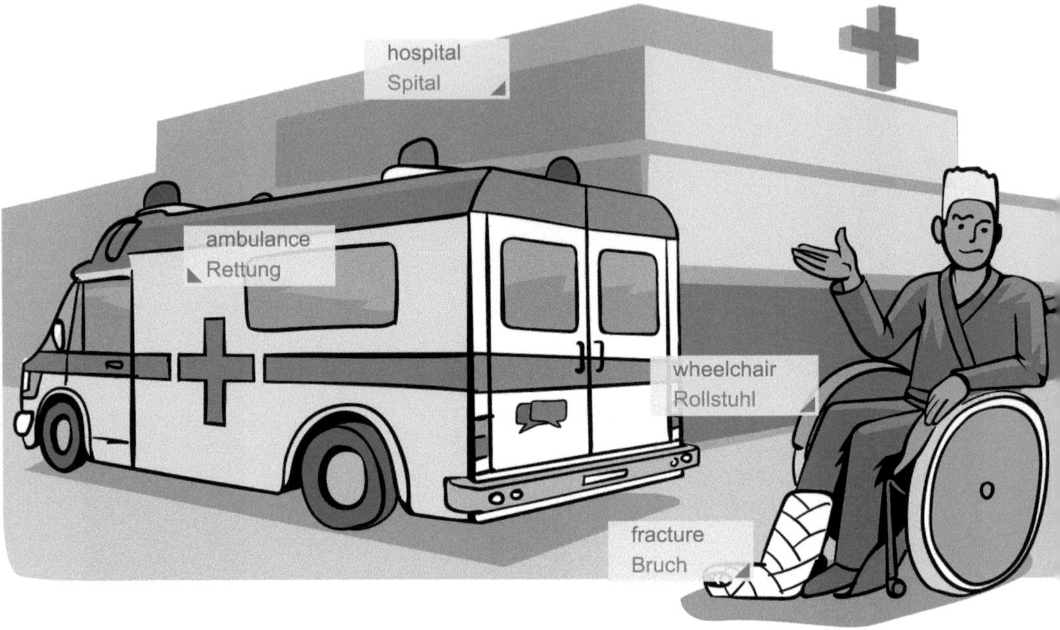

hospital
Spital
ambulance
Rettung
wheelchair
Rollstuhl
fracture
Bruch

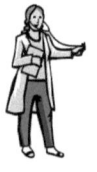

doctor

Ärztin

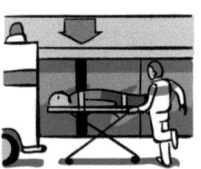

emergency room

Notaufnahme

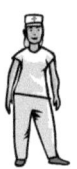

nurse

Krankenschwester

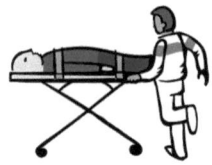

emergency

Notfall

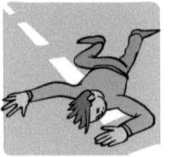

unconscious

ohnmächtig

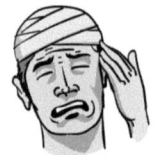

pain

Schmerz

injury

Verletzung

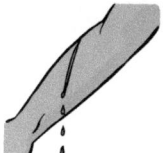

bleeding

Blutung

heart attack

Herzinfarkt

stroke

Schlaganfall

allergy

Allergie

cough

Husten

fever

Fieber

flu

Grippe

diarrhoea

Durchfall

headache

Kopfschmerzen

cancer

Krebs

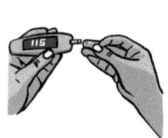

diabetes

Diabetes

surgeon

Chirurg

scalpel

Skalpell

operation

Operation

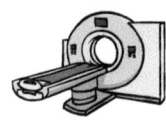

CT

CT

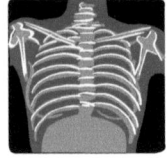

x-ray

Röntgen

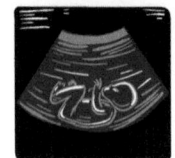

ultrasound

Ultraschall

face mask

Maske

disease

Krankheit

waiting room

Wartezimmer

crutch

Krücke

plaster

Pflaster

bandage

Verband

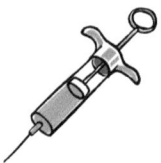

injection

Injektion

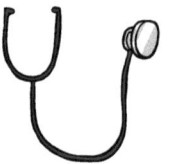

stethoscope

Stethoskop

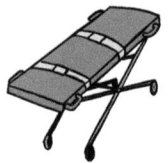

stretcher

Trage

clinical thermometer

Thermometer

birth

Geburt

overweight

Übergewicht

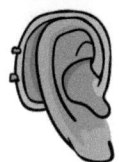

hearing aid

Hörgerät

disinfectant

Desinfektionsmittel

infection

Infektion

virus

Virus

HIV / AIDS

HIV / AIDS

medicine

Medizin

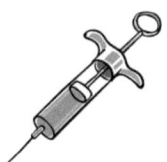

vaccination

Impfung

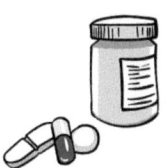

tablets

Tabletten

pill

Pille

emergency call

Notruf

blood pressure monitor

Blutdruckmesser

ill / healthy

krank / gesund

Help!
Hilfe!

alarm
Alarm

assault
Überfall

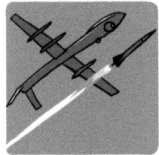

attack
Angriff

danger
Gefahr

emergency exit
Notausgang

Fire!
Feuer!

fire extinguisher
Feuerlöscher

accident
Unfall

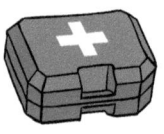

first-aid kit
Erste-Hilfe-Koffer

SOS
SOS

police
Polizei

Europe

Europa

North America

Nordamerika

South America

Südamerika

Africa

Afrika

Asia

Asien

Australia

Australien

Atlantic

Atlantik

Pacific

Pazifik

Indian Ocean

Indische Ozean

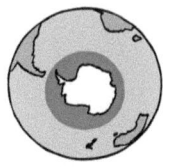

Antarctic Ocean

Antarktische Ozean

Arctic Ocean

Arktische Ozean

North Pole

Nordpol

South Pole
Südpol

Antarctica
Antarktis

Earth
Erde

land
Land

sea
Meer

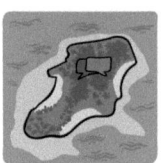

island
Insel

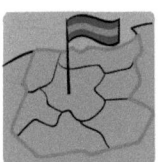

nation
Nation

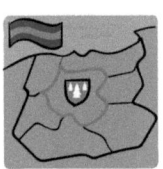

state
Staat

clock face

Ziffernblatt

hour hand

Stundenzeiger

minute hand

Minutenzeiger

second hand

Sekundenzeiger

What time is it?

Wie spät ist es?

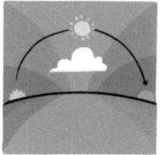

day

Tag

time

Zeit

now

jetzt

digital watch

Digitaluhr

minute

Minute

hour

Stunde

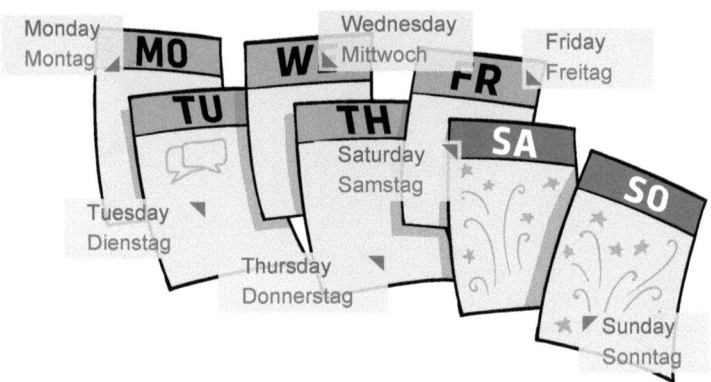

Monday
Montag

Wednesday
Mittwoch

Friday
Freitag

Tuesday
Dienstag

Thursday
Donnerstag

Saturday
Samstag

Sunday
Sonntag

yesterday

gestern

today

heute

tomorrow

morgen

morning

Morgen

noon

Mittag

evening

Abend

business days

Arbeitstage

weekend

Wochenende

rain
Regen

spring
Frühling

summer
Sommer

wind
Wind

autumn
Herbst

snow
Schnee

winter
Winter

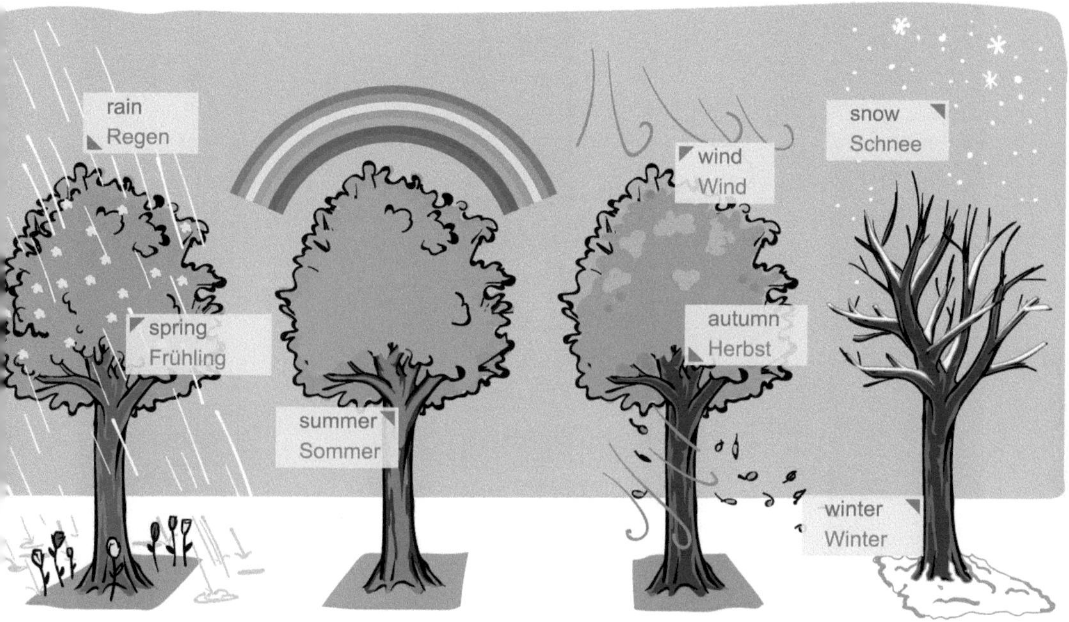

weather forecast

Wettervorhersage

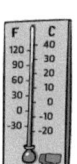

thermometer

Thermometer

sunshine

Sonnenschein

cloud

Wolke

fog

Nebel

humidity

Luftfeuchtigkeit

lightning

Blitz

thunder

Donner

storm

Sturm

hail

Hagel

monsoon

Monsun

flood

Flut

ice

Eis

January

Jänner

February

Februar

March

März

April

April

May

Mai

June

Juni

July

Juli

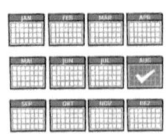

August

August

year - Jahr

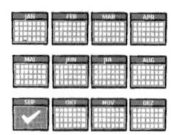

September
September

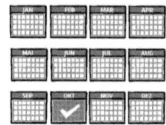

October
Oktober

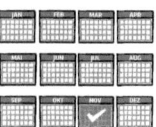

November
November

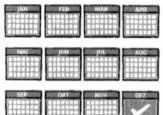

December
Dezember

shapes
Formen

circle
Kreis

square
Quadrat

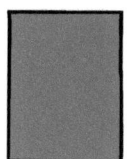

rectangle
Rechteck

triangle
Dreieck

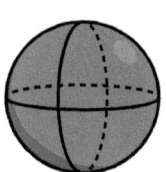

sphere
Kugel

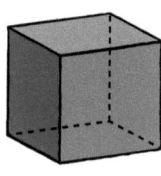

cube
Würfel

colours

Farben

white
·················
weiß

yellow
·················
gelb

orange
·················
orange

pink
·················
pink

red
·················
rot

purple
·················
lila

blue
·················
blau

green
·················
grün

brown
·················
braun

grey
·················
grau

black
·················
schwarz

a lot / a little

viel / wenig

angry / calm

wütend / friedlich

beautiful / ugly

hübsch / hässlich

beginning / end

Anfang / Ende

big / small

groß / klein

bright / dark

hell / dunkel

brother / sister

Bruder / Schwester

clean / dirty

sauber / schmutzig

complete / incomplete

vollständig / unvollständig

day / night

Tag / Nacht

dead / alive

tot / lebendig

wide / narrow

breit / schmal

edible / inedible

genießbar / ungenießbar

evil / kind

böse / freundlich

excited / bored

aufgeregt / gelangweilt

fat / thin

dick / dünn

first / last

zuerst / zuletzt

friend / enemy

Freund / Feind

full / empty

voll / leer

hard / soft

hart / weich

heavy / light

schwer / leicht

hunger / thirst

Hunger / Durst

ill / healthy

krank / gesund

illegal / legal

illegal / legal

intelligent / stupid

gescheit / dumm

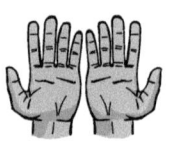

left / right

links / rechts

near / far

nah / fern

new / used
neu / gebraucht

nothing / something
nichts / etwas

old / young
alt / jung

on / off
an / aus

open / closed
offen / geschlossen

quiet / loud
leise / laut

rich / poor
reich / arm

right / wrong
richtig / falsch

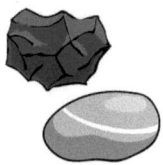

rough / smooth
rau / glatt

sad / happy
traurig / glücklich

short / long
kurz / lang

slow / fast
langsam / schnell

wet / dry
nass / trocken

warm / cool
warm / kühl

war / peace
Krieg / Frieden

0

zero

null

1

one

eins

2

two

zwei

3

three

drei

4

four

vier

5

five

fünf

6

six

sechs

7

seven

sieben

8

eight

acht

9

nine

neun

10

ten

zehn

11

eleven

elf

12

twelve

zwölf

13

thirteen

dreizehn

14

fourteen

vierzehn

15

fifteen

fünfzehn

16

sixteen

sechzehn

17

seventeen

siebzehn

18

eighteen

achtzehn

19

nineteen

neunzehn

20

twenty

zwanzig

100

hundred

hundert

1.000

thousand

tausend

1.000.000

million

Million

English
....
Englisch

American English
....
Amerikanisches Englisch

Chinese Mandarin
....
Chinesisch (Mandarin)

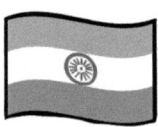

Hindi
....
Hindi

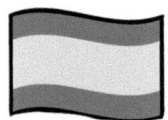

Spanish
....
Spanisch

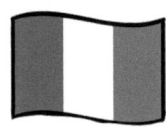

French
....
Französisch

Arabic
....
Arabisch

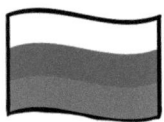

Russian
....
Russisch

Portuguese
....
Portugiesisch

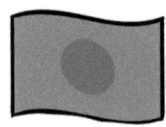

Bengali
....
Bengalisch

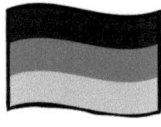

German
....
Deutsch

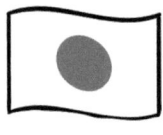

Japanese
....
Japanisch

I
ich

you
du

he / she / it
er / sie / es

we
wir

you
ihr

they
sie

who?
Wer?

what?
Was?

how?
Wie?

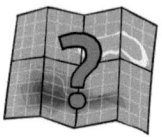

where?
Wo?

when?
Wann?

HELLO, I AM

name
Name

where

wo

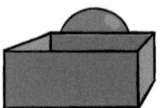

behind

hinter

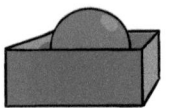

in

in

in front of

vor

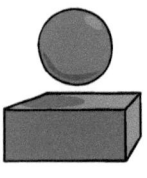

over

über

on

auf

under

unter

beside

neben

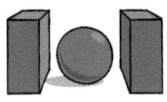

between

zwischen

place

Ort